It's a Crooked Road
but Not Far
to the House of Flowers

It's a Crooked Road
but Not Far
to the House of Flowers

Wendy Erd

A Publication of The Poetry Box®

Editing & Book Design by Shawn Aveningo Sanders
Cover Design by Robert R. Sanders
Cover Artwork by Diana Sanchez
Author Photo by Peter Kaufmann

ISBN: 978-1-956285-45-1
Library of Congress Control Number: 2023914337
Published in the United States of America.
Wholesale Distribution by Ingram Group

Published by The Poetry Box®, November 2023
Portland, Oregon
Website: thepoetrybox.com

for Peter

CONTENTS

Color Walk

When Almonds Bloom

You Are in The West

Lift the Lid of Thinking

At Times Be Still

Color Walk

Only by seeing such blue sky
Could I see how yellow
The plums were in the old man's hands.

The Window

A small box of darkness
opens into a dark
without edges.
Great horned owl's
five note call
freezes a rabbit,
white on whiter snow.
Up rises the predatory moon,
shadows blue the meadow.
Her mate hoots low
from the east and far below.

Sound has its own geography,
the heart a wide belonging.
We are not alone.

Woman in her window,
rabbits become snow,
owls' longing song.

Winter, a blueblack cape of stars
Pleiades, Taurus, Orion,
slowly turning towards dawn.

Elegy

1

All around us trees are dying quietly
their only broadcast a rain
of needles and the slow slub of resin.
For years we've come and gone,
lulled by their permanence,
their deep, cool shadow.

2

First the rain of tiny beetles.
Then the slow tick of needles dropping.
Tomorrow the forest will be cut down.

3

Before the sawyer comes
I rise early, pin a poem
to each dying tree.
You aren't making this easy.
Charlie reads each tree
before he hefts his saw
determines arc and fall
cuts the felling notch
drives in the final wedges.

4

Only stumps left.
The great spruce downed,
too much sky in their place.
The dark giants split into stove wood.
The forest has misplaced its shadow.
I will be old before they return.

* In 1997 a plague of spruce bark beetles, loosed by warming temperatures, decimated the spruce forests on Alaska's Kenai Peninsula

Rain

The space between
each drop, a loneliness,
grey in, grey out.

The porcupine
shakes it off,
twists his body,
let's quills
send comets of wet away.

Watching him,
I want to know
how to let loose
that way.

Spring Comes Up Like a Chrysler

Spring comes up like a Chrysler from a snowbank,
the antenna sprouts, slowly
the rest is revealed, chrome,
rusted chassis, bumpers bloom.

Beyond the bend a magpie
flutters up from the heap
of a winter-killed moose, its bill
half-filled with hair to pillow its nest.

In the wake of my neighbor's snowplow,
the breakup road drains its muddy chest.
Siberian squill pierce dark ice,
lift blue stars within reach.

Each spring,
the earth stutters,
and then, it sings.

A Form of Prayer

Under a shimmer of birch
a pattern of moose
bones on a low hill
signal winter claimed all
but the signature of her passing.

She holds her unborn still
in the white ark of her pelvis,
curl of spring moss on tiny scapulae,
nagoonberries embrace her twins
in a green upwelling, a hymn.

Let me surrender
with this same grace
to a process as inevitable
as snow covering starvation
or berries ripening
against bone.

The Price of Fish

My moods shift like the July sky, first brilliant
then dark, intensified by the constant wind.
The Alaska Peninsula flattens and narrows
here by this muddy river, where the weather's
driven restless as a mad woman,
running her hand through rumpled hair
impassioned by both the Gulf of Alaska and the Bering Sea.

I rest in bed just below my body,
the hands folded on my chest, not mine,
but orphans.
The husk of myself.
Deadened muscles in my wrists and forearms
ache with a season of fishing.
Left alone, my fingers curl
around an invisible salmon.
We've pulled thousands from our nets.

I twist on a mooring in bed and feel the tug of the current,
though our cabin sits in the tundra above the tide.
The few hours of sleep erase the boundaries of both land and time.
My crew calls me "Queen of Tides" as
I chalk a relentless schedule on the wall.
One more week and the run will be over.

Two days ago, a storm threw windrows
of jellyfish high on the beach,
dry rubbery circles with brown stripes.
They catch in our nets and billow like circus tents.

[. . .]

Flotsam of sea and tide surge
with the stench of dead fish,
bloated ghosts of red salmon that
reek of decay and litter the tide lines,
summoning both brown bear and gull.
The grass has long since gone to seed.
Everything hurries toward winter
in the long light of summer,
spewing progeny, then dying.

I don't recognize my face in the mirror,
an old woman stares back at me.
My eyes are pinched with wrinkles and
my white hair's whipped coarse by the wind.
The season's pulled me into itself and
I can no longer resist.

Pilot Point, Alaska, July 24

Wallflowers

Beached boats like dowagers
without pensions,
wooden ribs sprung, petticoats upended,
wind-rouged and sagging,
double chinned and chested,
wallflowers waiting,
hull heavy in the weeds,
for some kind captain
to ask them to dance.

Summer's Last Swimmer

Some would say fall's decay
is summer's last swimmer,
the crook of an arm
disappearing in the green
grass bent with rain.

Gathering Footprints

After we die, we gather every footprint we've taken.
          —Zeng Qingxin

When I gather every footprint
I'll return here
to the dry course of a river
that changed its mind.
Wosnesenski
Unatkuyuk
Its native tongue… ice water, sweepers, stones.
Its language… hurry here, hurry there,
meander.

All morning we follow its traces
among smoothed stones,
collect shoots of cottonwood
to bonsai later in a Chinese bowl.

Lunch on a dry bank with
old friends. Cups of black tea.
An ant scribes granite,
each step a day,
years to cross over.

Returning home our boat
scatters rafts of murrelets,
now black, now white
skimming an origami sea.

Mantilla

In town each night at dusk,
after a day of humble scrounging,
a lace of crows flies back across the bay to roost,
black stitching on winter's sky
the finest threads of home.

The Shape of Listening

Outside the conference hall
beyond long windows
just offshore, something black surfaces.

Not dolphins at all but round rock
rising as the tide drops,
black backed and slippery.

In the distance,
two figures trace an isthmus of sand.
Inside, we're adrift.

A drone of speakers,
words wrapping words
drowsy with sleep.

From the mist
two sandhill cranes
fly by, low and slow.

With a few wild beats,
from the far side of sound,
their trailing song

opens wide and round
the shape of our listening,
and the wakened world comes rushing in.

When Almonds Bloom

When almonds bloom in spring,
there's a haiku in the orchard.

Laundry of Hours

Waking alone
I held you
as one must
bookmark a dream
or suspend an edge of air
above the hem of rising water
folding the hours
against your absence.

Walking aimlessly
I roamed a city
when an apple tree,
bright with bloom,
and heady with blossom,
swept me into its arms.

Below that lacework
of sky and flower
the heart's door slid open.

It wasn't that
I missed you less

It was that
there was less of me

and more
of the world
in its place.

Bertie Creek

What happens when we have
only charcoal from the edge of the campfire
and an envelope to write on?

We read poems aloud
between threads of smoke.
One line reminds you of a story
you wrote in third grade,
not what it was about,
only that it was pages long.

Each day could begin this way
with simple tools.
Poems threaded with bird song,
morning smoke making a mirage of early air,
you drifting backwards, floating forwards
line after line, no end in sight.

What Our Bodies Know

Our bodies make up long before we do.
Frumped apart by argument, icy cold
in bed, each to our own edge,
then the warm arch of you
seeks the length of me
and we intertwine like vines
holding each other from falling
into all that darkness.

The Blue Hour

Copenhagen, and the blue hour is here.
Silently, the puppeteer watches
dusk deepen, light stars.
His kind hands busy with making.
Under his workbench a wicker basket
of sock dolls keep him companion.
In the blue hour.

From rooftops, cats and laundry
come down, curl and fold
by first floor stoves.
The roar of day returns to river sounds.

Night finds indigo.
Down come shades.
Are secrets good for a marriage
in the blue hour?

In Copenhagen
at dawn, a pair of swans.
At dusk, the puppeteer.
In the cobblestone darkness,
behind a sign, Closed For The Night
a couple, not caring at all
how transparent glass is,
Kiss. And kiss.

At Night Above Our Sleep

~for Peter

I meet you in the air

barefoot and supple
carrying a basket of memories and leaves,
the one you gave
when you fell for me,
the one you took back,
a forest of leaves,
green clocks that turn the wind.

Now autumn, the stacked
spruce of days waits to be split,
become fire,
the hush of spring,
paintbox and promise,
asleep under snow.

After seasons
waking beside you,
our old eyes soften
to blur beautiful
the familiar of
so many years.

The Addition

It is this,
creating beauty
in the last room
we will share,
soft floors of madrone,
amber light.
Imagining spaces for infirmity,
when only our eyes
will hold each other
above the drift of days.

I Hope I'm Folding Chairs
When I'm Ninety

~for Marge Mullen

Old Marge folds them easily as cloth napkins
after her daughter's poetry reading.
Space in the room growing, laughter and talk
taking the place of leaned in listening.

Is it ninety years that makes Marge so enviable?
Or the way she moves, flipping seats closed,
stacking them in neat rows against the wall
like cordwood, like years she's counted and put aside.

Or might it be the way she raised her daughter Mary,
nearing sixty, who writes her own daughter into our lives.
Little Lilly, her eleven-year-old "adopted Irish miracle"
beams at her mother from the front row.

Later I catch Mary touching her mother's cheek
after the reading. Her hand lingers.
Then Marge is gone folding chairs again. Making space.
As the best of mothers do for their daughters.

Confluence and Curves

A crowd pools in morning fog
around three blind palm readers
on an arched bridge in Chengdu
where everything curves,
the river, the girl's back
damp beneath her wooden yoke,
the wheeled stream of bikes passing.

On the crowd's edge an old man
rotates three silver balls
in one hand behind his back, round
and round and round, balanced as planets.

Seers, eclipsed moons where your eyes
should be, what do you see in your darkness
when you spread flat the palm, unfold the map
of the heart, trace a line of wisdom, of fate,
 of life hurrying around the thumb's hump?

I should've stopped, though I didn't speak your language.
I feared your predications, their weight.
Now I could use such soothsaying,
my hands hold rivers without destination.

I stand alone by the sink
washing my hands,
my mother's hands,
my grandmother's hands,
the white moons in my pink nails
rising for the third time in a century of women
washing dishes and staring out windows.

Spent Glories

Morning glories bear large blue, pink, and white flowers which open in the morning and gradually fade during the day.
—*Ipomoea purpurea* seed packet

It's a crooked road, but not far,
to the house of flowers.

Vines on a childhood fence,
cerulean trumpets, so blue,
you understood "wistful"
before you had that word.

Tendrils curl, climb telephone wires,
twist like a girl's damp hair
on the nape of her neck on a hot summer's day.
Blossoms soften afternoons into
the blue hour of evening.

Susie Irwin in Cheshire, Oregon sells morning glories,
eighty-four seeds to the packet. From her photo on the back
she looks like she'd bake peach pies
not harvest acres of pods clattering in a fall wind.

Susie is loosing her bloom,
from the looks of it,
dimples curve above the drape of her chin.

[. . .]

In the women's bathhouse we know
who is coming into glory
and who is fading.
Spent blossoms bob
past tight buds
about to unfurl every note
in the scale of blue.

Tassajara, May 2014

You Are in the West

You are in the West
I am in the East
How immense the Pacific Ocean
But our hearts have a common rhythm
I offer to you, Wendy, this grace.

—Bà (Grandmother) Thục
Hà Nội, Việt Nam

Sài Gòn If Only

~for Phương Mai

Mai calls me *Cô Tiên*
the fairy who offers dreams.

Were that I could grant
such simple desires

The Moon-Faced Prostitute
would find the Kind-Eyed man.
Loneliness would roar off on a
late model motorbike
and never look back.

The addicted son would return
and cover his mother
asleep on the sidewalk
outside Chợ Lớn market.

Đi and Xa nhà, "Go" and her baby, "Far From Home,"
would travel the river home to Cambodia,
to rice-field, mango-tree, water-jar,
lamp-light, home, husband.

The black canal would shake loose its garbage cloak,
wear only lotus blossoms.
The old couple curled in their sampan
would smell salt air and sleep.

Children of the street, would remember they were children.

Full, the moon would understand.
Satisfied, the dark night
would bestow silver.

Just Beyond Us

Minh dreams he is a boy again
swimming into a mirror of small
waves on Ho Ngọc Hà.

Now an old rubber shoe drifts
in the tangle of lilies
that swallow the pond.

I dream my unborn children
into my arms,

color seeps back
into my white hair.

Just beyond us,
night rearranges

the impossible.

Our Students Translate Their Names

Miss Miracles Come True
Mrs. Perfumed Grass
Mrs. Distant Rain
Mrs. Autumn Water
Mrs. Womanly Peace
Miss Mysterious
Mr. Sunlight
Mr. Long River
Mr. Prosperity
Mr. Light of Happiness

Hà Nội, Việt Nam, 2008

An Old Man Waltzes Past
While We Practice Taiji

~for Teacher Vinh

Beneath a rain-wet willow, the green pond,
Indra's jeweled net scribed drop by drop.

On the slick path an old man waltzes
in the mist, alone under his umbrella.

Thầy Vinh lifts crane wings, soft as air
Buddha-eyes half closed, he gently
turns the universe, in perfect balance,
a man bird, a breath wing.

Hà Nội Botanical Garden, Việt Nam

Mosaic

A mosaic is a conversation with time
—Terry Tempest Williams

Maybe all farewells go like this.

After twenty years
I'm leaving Việt Nam
but pretend otherwise.
Say, *we'll meet again*, just
as the door clicks closed.

The streets are waking.
Sweep of twig broom, cock's crow,
Bánh cuốn broth rising.
From his basket a young man
sells me a hand of ripe bananas
for the last time.
On the small bridge
temple flags fly for the black Buddha
in Trúc Bạch's temple.

These will continue on,
if I were to stay. If I left.

Today, I will step out of this life
as thoroughly as the north wind
that last night lifted loose leaves
to mosaic the street below with color
leaving space behind for morning light.

Nearing Midnight in Green Lake Park

~for Yang Kun

The moon
one perfect white circle
above the old bridge.

Three arches float
their mirrored halves
in water below.

One bright above
Three dark below

Tea shops closed
The bridge empty
The night full

Only my footsteps
to accompany me.

Kunming, China

Salt Looks Like Sugar

There's no English at the grocery
in Kunming, salt looks like sugar.
Girl without tongue, I thread through this city of millions.

The air smells of coal, the wind seeks all corners.
All rivers rush to borders, all borders meet,
except mine, which I left at home in a suitcase under the bed.

Next-door cats prowl the upcurved roof
of the last old house in the alley. Down the street,
the old woman with bound feet sits on a bench in late sun.
I long to hear her story, her face a folded map, a dried plum.
I don't know how to know my neighbors.

In cafés I sit alone at tables. From shop windows
my reflection peers, white haired and lanky.
I am a nun of circumstance, isolate, yet strangely happy.

Each morning I jog through Green Lake Park
where near dawn women carve the sky with swords,
Mao-capped men play cards, their caged birds sing.
Harmony rises early in this blue-sky city of eternal spring.

One night a man let me peer through his telescope,
I swear the moon looked Chinese.
What did I ever really know of Kunming?
Only the heart felt pull of an erhu's string.

All I knew was what I felt,
elusive as sugar dissolved in tea.
Memory folded like an origami rose
paper thin and sweet.

Kunming's Morning Market

Later, I remembered
the drumming rain and
I pictured her
peddling in from a far village
her bike baskets full of flowers in the early darkness
the quick heavy downpour
ruining her day's work.

And I wondered why
I didn't stop to buy
the bruised yellow lilies
she'd held out to me
in the market.

Waiting

Nervous Japanese Await Quake
—Anchorage Daily News

In Ito, along the fiery rim,
the children leave early
walking in pairs to school
their black lacquer boxes carefully packed with
rice, turnip pickles and a finger of fish.

All day the women sweep red maple leaves
against the wind with twig brooms.

Way after dusk their husbands shush in on the rails,
grim faced men on the Shinkansen
with more work than the red sun
will allow in one day.
They stop at the makeshift bars on the street
and steady themselves with a drink.

In the shadows of the wooden temple,
heedless of the trembling earth,
a monk prunes the pine's needles
into a perfect arrangement of space.

And though it's only October,
the old man up the dark valley
dreams of December
when he will hang his white daikons to dry
like icicles from his thick thatched roof
and watch for the persimmons
like orange moons to ripen
into sweet globes on his skeletal tree.

The Weavers of Fate

All night in Sam Tai
the click-clack of shuttled thread.
One bulb lights the women's looms.

Weave this pattern:
The edge of the past
indigo to crimson to foreigners coming.
The finest weavers in Laos
run to bring us their cloth.

Weave this pattern:
Red road that scars the jungle,
one bus a day, five miles an hour.
The Lao bus driver and my American husband
speak together in Vietnamese.
Weave patterns of tiger, snake, mouse, frog.
Shimmer of a Laotian temple. Its bells.

Weave tradition, weave war.
Weave the sounds of shuttle
and all-night roosters,
the indigo darkness and stars.
Above its weft, weave the girl
who walked six days from Vietnam
to find a husband.
Weave in the Japanese curator
hunting for weavings to buy.
Weave in her questions: *Wild forest chickens?*
The name of the place?
Weave in the villagers' curiosity, their hunger,
their smiles and their stares.

Weave in the wild far side of the river
too steep to slash, green thread
and the old trees texture
across the raw edge of silk.

This cloth could be an ordinary skirt
worn to the rice fields.
Its hem fifty years of history
or five hundred years of song.

What pattern now?
An old man's face, ochre and sienna,
earth toned above an indigo jacket.

The cloth is a journey
the weight of it long.
The curator asks,
How much silk on the scale?

The shuttle's thrown once more,
from the jungle, emerges the taste of civet cat.

This is the cloth of the weavers of fate:
       This man has no eye.
       I have a wallet of kip.
       She has a large basket of greens.
       Those boys throw wooden tops
       that spin in the dirt school yard.
       That baby runs down the village road.
       Each thread, pulled tightly and bound.

Sam Tai, Xam Neua, Laos 2003

Lift the lid of thinking,
underneath is the whole sky.

In Bhutan

When it snows, crows and children sing.
Under the moon, a leopard crosses Dochula,
her prints a five petaled poem.
Tomorrow, only road and wind.
Above the nunnery, pines gather snowflakes
with slim green fingers,
tonight they'll wear diamonds.
There is no beginning or end
to a sky such as this.

Undone, I wish I knew the secret of staying
or the gift of falling slow.

Return

A lone tree white with blossom
Mountains fall toward blue
Ridges recede into evening sky
Whose sable brush strokes this softly?
I count horizons home
Soon we'll be gone
The road wet with rain.

Bumthang Valley, Bhutan

Acupuncture

~for Ellen

I lie still on the table,
punctured by delicate needles,
and imagine tiny beams of light
filtering along the meridians.
Like headlights of lost cars,
they travel dark roads,
searching for home.

From This Height

Flying over the Cascades
the mountain's blue spine
funnels the smoke
of a hundred fires,
their char and loss and ache.
From this height
only a Chinese scroll,
inked ridge beyond ridge,
bone after bone.
What can such cold
beauty teach?

Rain At Last

~after hearing the news of Thích Nhất Hạnh's stroke
November 2014

On the clothesline
an empty coat hanger
gathers a necklace,
tiny diamonds hanging
on in the wind.

Even now parched
meadows on Mt. Tam
roll towards green
disbelieving drought,
shaking off the news
with each cool rivulet.

Redwoods, steady with time,
stand taller, show us
what old hands
they are at patience.

Along the Path at Tassajara

Blossoms lift their hands
from leaves,
one pinecone placed
as sentinel on a stone.

Nothing is lost here.
A pocket stone found again
on the front stoop.

Footprints fill each other
coming and going.

Red ants cross
a path's raked ridges,
gravel spirals the task
of grounding, of placement.

Walking the Beauty Road
objects teach us
to transform obstacles.
The snake's rattles,
tiny shoji screens.

Each stop on the path
is a soft voice proffering.

Bees speak in exhalations
of lavender, as they rise
fall and rise again above
a drift of purple blossoms
that lead to the Zendo.

At the Dolmen

In the grass, golden mirrors.
In my feet, doorways.
In my hands, fire.

Rocamadour, France

Whereabouts

We are on the line 157 337... running on line north and south.
    —Amelia Earhart's last radio transmission
    July 2, 1937

Green troughs become
dark froth rolled under.
Bearings dissolve,
in every direction, ocean.

On land we orient on waves of lilac and wind.
Grass seeded along the roadway grew overnight,
this morning small blades ripple.

What can we chart?
Pollen dusts our thresholds gold,
makes ordinary doorways sacred.

An unfathomable radiance moves through us,
we are more of this world than we know, and less.

Body of light seeping across time ...

Broadcast these whereabouts,
send this news.

On Buddha's Birthday

On the full moon in May a robin sings,
though the light has long since faded.

Even as the moon whispers *midnight*,
that robin's song enters my open window.

Too happy to fall asleep
I sing without sound
as I lie in
a round circle
of light.

Prairie of Days

Let wheels roll west
toward an unknown edge,
stacks of what we once possessed
left behind in neat pyramids of memory.

Those that burdened,
those not necessary.
With a long gaze back,
those most precious.

Stuff of days, jettisoned.
Beside grandmother's china,
outgrown shoes in pairs.
Further on a heap of unspent dreams.

Youth unravels a fine white line
leaking like flour from a pinpoint hole
across the prairie of days
until the sack is empty.
Beauty, its twin,
left shimmering.

Yet more to give.
Every loved atom.
Even grief must go.

Unhitched, on a green hill,
the calm scatter
of your own bleached bones.

All falls away. No matter.
One moment there,
the next only forest and field.

To the west
an evening star lingers
above the long blue lap of the sea.

At Times Be Still

Beluga Slough Poems

Thanks Be to Beluga Slough

For ebbing and flooding without a hitch
for mixing salt and sweet
for sedges with edges
for a cirque of calm
in the center of town
for green-winged teal, eagles, mink tracks, mink,
sticklebacks, fairy shrimp
for rust red mud and
puddles' rainbow sheen
for brush strokes of coal where tide rolls
out and every shade of green
for grasses that map the margin of salt,
arrowgrass, goosetongue, silverweed
for the singles club of sandhill cranes
flap dancing on a bar in mud-rosy preen
for disappearing acts each fall,
return of song come spring
for all who migrate
north, south, east and west
footed, finned and feathered
for those who come
and leave sustained
Thanks be.

April: Migrating Birds Month*

After the month Bear Turns Over
After it's Getting Light Again
When we've worn winter
like an old coat far too long

From emptiness, from air
Come wings and song.

Landing in the marsh grass,
Dabbling in the mud,
Feeding in the sedges.

We count them in like old friends,
Pintail's silhouette,
Raucous yellow legs,
Sky-whistling snipe.
Sandpipers flash by
A gossip of speckled-chested geese.
Sky-hinges, the rust-rattle cries of sandhill cranes
Pry open windows and doors

They're back!!!

We telegraph the town
Lifted by this surge—
Life driven with longing
Against all odds.
From darkness to light,
From silence to song.

*English translation of the Dena'ina names for the months of April, December, and January.

Advice from an Estuary

Look ordinary,
Don't ask for much.
Travel to your edge, then go further.
Empty out.
Let the moon refill you.
Embrace opposites easily.
Host travelers without borders, feed them,
Listen to the distance in their songs.
Nurture the invisible, harbor the young.
Send those you've raised out into the world.
Digest insults. Reframe and cleanse them.
Adopt silence while others speak all around you.
Measure change calmly.
Mirror the sky.
At times,
Be still.

Time Lives Differently Here

Time lives differently here
Tucked behind a storm berm
Beside the blue hinge of the sea.

Clock of waters drawn by the moon
In and out, out and in,
The estuary's gently breathing.

Mud flat, channels, tufted plain
Soon, a sedge-rimmed pewter lake.
Quick print of a mink, washed away by tide.

History stacks time like driftwood in the slough
Tales of woolly mammoth pass by knee-deep in ooze,
Eons of migrant birds, calendars of song,
Sea otter hunters off Bishops Beach,
Seldovia's boat, the Copper, tows in a loaded scow.

Or just now

A little boy skips stones
across the outlet
as if all that mattered
was the moment between
each weightless bounce.

As a last slant of sun
lifts the edge of what we know
to turn the marsh grass gold.

Listening for the Rain

Everyday is like this,
the short and long of forgetting:
a man with a walking stick, a limp,
his daughter in a red sweatshirt,
crossing the berm.

Ten years from now
will they remember
that the beach they walked
smelled of rain,
that drops made small ticks
on his ballcap,
feathers on cheeks, set
diamonds in her hair?

If we could remember not only the rain
but the weight of the damp jacket,
not only the jacket but the ease
our bodies have moving through time
beside another
without the word why.
On a cold, salt-wet afternoon,
the vapor of our breath
rising ahead of us
trailing behind.

ACKNOWLEDGMENTS

Many thanks to the editors & publishers, writing contest judges, composers, musicians, and others who previously published, or celebrated in their own way, these poems:

Anchorage Daily News 15th Annual Creative Writing Contest 1996 (First Place Open Poetry & Grand Prize): "Waiting"

Alaska State Council on the Arts, National Poetry Month selection 2006: "The Blue Hour"

Bunnell Steet Arts Center and ArtPlace America, Beluga Slough Trail Poems 2013: "Thanks Be to Beluga Slough,""Advice from an Estuary,""April: Migrating Birds Month," "Time Lives Differently Here," and "Listening for the Rain"

Cirque (Vol. 6, No. 1, 2015): "At Night above Our Sleep" and "Gathering Footprints"

Cirque (Vol. 8, No. 1, 2016): "A Form of Prayer"

Fairbanks Arts Association Statewide Poetry Contest, 2022 (First Place): "Whereabouts"

Homer News, Kenai Peninsula Writer's Contest 1994 (First Place Poetry): "The Price of Fish"

New Music Composition 2018, Larry Moss, composer: "Advice from An Estuary"

Tell Me Your Story: A Four-Part Series, spoken word with video production and original music scored and played by Hal McMillen (halmcmillen.com): "Advice from an Estuary" and "Listening for the Rain"

With gratitude to Tulku Yeshi Rinpoche who once asked, "What kind of a postman would they be if they received letters but never delivered them? Deliver the letters!" At last, here they are. And with deep thanks to Kim Stafford, Emily Wall, Naomi Shihab Nye, Hal McMillen, Diana Sanchez, and Peter Kaufmann for sage advice and for always cheering me on.

EARLY PRAISE

So many moments I had to look away toward the horizon and let a poem settle in my heart.

—Kim Stafford, author of *Singer Come from Afar*

The profound inversions of the senses in Wendy Erd's poems *drifting backwards, floating forwards* guide us with deft reverence to see more of this world than we knew we knew.

—Lady Borton, author,
After Sorrow: An American Among the Vietnamese

Beautiful, gorgeous book! Wendy Erd's words have always had spirit-cleansing power. She abides in such intimate relation to everything, spruce trees of Alaska, porcupines, snow, a packet of morning-glory seeds, a Kunming grocery, a long loving relationship, inevitable aging—that her spare phrases and stanzas all feel like deep home. Each day could begin this way/ with simple tools. These poems are exquisite compasses to live by.

—Naomi Shihab Nye, author,
Everything Comes Next: Collected & New Poems

ABOUT THE AUTHOR

For twenty years, Wendy Erd traveled between Alaska and Asia supporting indigenous and seldom heard communities to voice their stories through exhibit and film. Now at home in Alaska, mornings begin in front of the wood stove with coffee, a stack of poetry books and her husband as they read poems aloud to begin each day.

Her writing appears as prose on road signs in Alaska's Copper River watershed and as poems along an estuary trail in Homer, Alaska. She's received several statewide literary awards. Her work has been published by the *Anchorage Daily News, Alaska Quarterly Review, New Rivers Press, Cirque*, and anthologized in *Out on the Deep Blue: Women, Men and the Ocean They Fish*. In collaboration with her dear friend, Lê Phương, their poetry translations were published in *The Defiant Muse: Vietnamese Feminist Poems from Antiquity to the Present*. She envisioned and coordinated *Poems in Place*, a project that placed poetry by Alaskan poets on signs in Alaska's state parks.

About The Poetry Box®

The Poetry Box,® a boutique publishing company in Portland, Oregon, provides a platform for both established and emerging poets to share their words with the world through beautiful printed books and chapbooks.

Feel free to visit the online bookstore (thePoetryBox.com), where you'll find more titles including:

The Round Whisper of No Moon by Peter Kaufmann

Tracking the Fox by Rosalie Sanara Petrouske

Elemental Things by Michael S. Glaser

Listening in the Dark by Suzy Harris

When All Else Fails by Lana Hechtman Ayers

Earthwork by Kristin Berger

Jump Straight Up by Jarold Ramsey

A Nest in the Heart by Vivienne Popperl

The Catalog of Small Contentments by Carolyn Martin

The Hills Are Dust and Light by Karen Gookin

The Call Home by Susan Johnson

Quilting the Loose Edges by Susan Woods Morse

Tell Her Yes by Ann Farley

This Is the Lightness by Rachel Barton

and more . . .